ANTHONY WAKEFIELD HILL

THE REAL MOTIVES FOR SCOTTISH AND CATALAN INDEPENDENCE

The Myth of Freedom

ANTHONY WAKEFIELD HILL

THE REAL MOTIVES FOR SCOTTISH AND CATALAN INDEPENDENCE

The Myth of Freedom

MEREO
Cirencester

Mereo Books

1A The Wool Market Dyer Street Cirencester Gloucestershire GL7 2PR
An imprint of Memoirs Publishing www.mereobooks.com

The Real Motives for Scottish and Catalan Independence

ISBN: 978-1-86151-885-9

First published in Great Britain in 2018
by Mereo Books, an imprint of Memoirs Publishing

The address for Memoirs Publishing Group Limited can be found at
www.memoirspublishing.com

The Memoirs Publishing Group Ltd Reg. No. 7834348

The Memoirs Publishing Group supports both The Forest Stewardship Council® (FSC®) and the PEFC® leading international forest-certification organisations. Our books carrying both the FSC label and the PEFC® and are printed on FSC®-certified paper. FSC® is the only forest-certification scheme supported by the leading environmental organisations including Greenpeace. Our paper procurement policy can be found at www.memoirspublishing.com/environment

Typeset in 12/18pt Century Schoolbook
by Wiltshire Associates Publisher Services Ltd. Printed and bound in Great Britain by Printondemand-Worldwide, Peterborough PE2 6XD

CONTENTS

Foreword

About the Author

Published Titles by Anthony Wakefield Hill

Preface

FOREWORD

The significance of relations between the Individual and the Whole cannot be overestimated, in respect of everything from metaphysics to politics, and it has particular relevance today in view of the tensions created by the many individual groups clamouring for independence in an *essentially interdependent world;* the unity of the Whole is paramount, and everyone is someone's servant – a thing that needs to be considered by all those independence-craving egoists and nationalistic xenophobes.

The obvious solution to the Catalonian crisis, and many others, is for independence to be achieved *within unity* – the unity, in this case, of the overall Spanish nation, or overall Spanish government. There is no rational need for outright and complete independence, such an outcome being determined by pure conceit and arrogance, pushing the whole agenda to the point of civil war.

At all costs let there be dialogue, for both the nationalists and the Spanish government are obliged, as civilised citizens, to adopt diplomacy. Of course the Spanish state cannot allow absolute independence in its midst, and the Catalans, if their cause has any justification at all, must have a hearing.

The question of *Tibetan* independence should also be mentioned, the Dalai Llama himself having recommended that the overall unity of Chinese rule should remain, while the verbal struggle for tolerance and *religious* freedom should persist; let us hope it proves true that the pen is mightier than the sword.

ABOUT THE AUTHOR

The author is reputed amongst a large section of the public to be the twenty-first century Christian prophet, despite some healthy personal doubt, on his part, that serves to prove his sanity; preferring to be known as a purely human prophet, retaining the name of Anthony Hill, he finds his own salvation, as well as man's, in the writing of this series of books – the creative 'stream of consciousness'.

Published Titles by Anthony Wakefield Hill

All the author's books are to be found under Amazon Books and Lulu, on the Internet, a list of forthcoming titles – written though as yet unpublished – being included at the rear of this volume.

PREFACE

Alex Salmond and other Scots have decided, like naughty little schoolboys, that independence for Scotland would be a wizard wheeze, for no better reason than a romantic attempt to strike a dramatic pose in the world and at the same time score a few points off old England. These, and other motives, which would never be admitted, are the subliminal forces behind this desire for self-glorification, projected on a national scale, in which politics and economics are an ill-disguised front.

Independence for Scotland is an illusion; it can never come about. Scotland is tied militarily, economically, politically and socially to its English neighbours, from whom it cannot disassociate itself – in particular, psychologically; the Scottish and English mentalities – and, for that matter, the Welsh – have become welded together historically into a common psyche; it is this psychological unity more than any other that forms the indissoluble identity of the United Kingdom.

The personal proclivities of Alex Salmond, and a few other malcontents, must not be allowed to lead the nation any further astray than his talent for rabble-rousing has already succeeded in doing.

Half the Scottish nation resides in England; if independence comes, are all those Scots going to bugger off back to Scotland, leaving their businesses behind them? If I were the British, or English, government I would place an embargo on all Scottish business interests in this country; if they want independence, let them practise it in their own homeland. The fact that they could retaliate by freezing English assets in Scotland only goes to prove the absolutely mutual dependence and indissoluble ties of our two economies. To be independent in the true sense of the word, Scotland would have to withdraw all its historically-established interests, whether personal or economic, from south of the border. Oh, Salmond says, we can be independent without all that! Can they? This simian excuse for a mind simply has not thought things out; Salmond himself wants Scotland to be truly independent: that is his whole intention – to do England in the eye; unspoken but true – but is such an independence worth having, with half your people, your personal affiliations, and half your commercial assets, being based in England, furthermore sharing a military alliance – of which the English would bear most of the burden – and celebrating an intricately mutual culture? Is this unbreachable and indispensable reciprocity really independence?

In the political and psychological climate of the world today, any attempt at the disintegration of political union is potentially disastrous – a retrograde step. The only way forward for modernity is integration, and more integration; nationalistic movements, whether political or military, are almost always unjustifiable – particularly when the motives are egoistic and racist. The only authentic desire for freedom would be in the event of political or military oppression, and then only rarely; far better to rely on peaceful protest and civil disobedience, however long it takes. Impatience must be curbed.

The idea that Scotland is a place where people are stronger, braver or more intelligent than the English – commonly held by Scots, though unconsciously – and that therefore its people should not tolerate any association with English folk, which is the *underlying* basis of the desire for separation, is of course ethically indefensible. The belief, also current in Scotland, that the Argyll and Sutherland Highlanders could knock spots off the English Army, is untenable: they couldn't get their

John Thomases up any higher than the Queen's Own Dragoon Guards.

Independence for Scotland is a chimera.

*****

What I have to say, I say in the interests of truth and United Kingdom unity, and, ultimately, world peace.

Take a look at the face of Alex Salmond, and then at the face of Nicola Sturgeon; for they both reveal in large measure the psychological motives behind the urge to Scottish independence. In them is encapsulated the less savoury characteristics of the Scots nationalists as a whole; allowing for individual differences there is sufficient evidence in their leaders' faces of the strident ego and general self-congratulation of the average bog-trotting Celt, accompanied by its habitual surly and guttural vocalisation.

Salmond's features are expressive of a crude and bumptious egoism, smug in its conviction that it is appointed above all others to rule – a belief no doubt incurred after Salmond's unfortunate romantic involvement (with an Englishwoman) that ended in rejection; what does such a primitive and powerful ego do in these circumstances but reject, in turn, the former object of its affections, and anything associated with her, including her nationality? This obvious reason for Salmond's disaffection and resulting demand for independence has been pointed out before by an unusually perceptive writer, but was, of course, blithely ignored; look to the psyche, hidden within, for the true causes of our external drives and embroilments – especially the xenophobia that we all harbour – and do not doubt the overwhelming power of the repercussions generated by an apparently small personal setback or rebuff.

If you Scots do not believe these disclosures, assuming to the contrary that your leader's character, unfortunately representative of your own, is not so fickle or petty or suggestible, then I suggest you take a long, hard look at both him and yourselves in the light of our pathetic human psychology, before you swallow any more of his facile and persuasive spiel.

Nicola Sturgeon, her visage seething with spite and resentment against the convenient scapegoat across the border – though she manages to disguise her motives – suffers from an almost insanely inflated self-love, betrayed by her swaggering head, as she delivers her tirades, and by her excessively confident attitude; a confidence born of unshakeable self-justification and resolute belief in the wickedness of her foe. Who has done this to you, Nicola? Some member of your family, someone at school – at work? Whoever it was certainly made a lasting impression. And under it all lies a deep feeling of inferiority, giving rise to an egoistic search for a target onto which to deflect the smarting pain.

I do not doubt her astuteness as a politician, but I shudder at that cold and deadly voice, that smouldering gaze, in the service of a calculating malevolence, a consuming jealousy of the establishment and those in a more fortunate position – which is acquired in most cases by diligence, intelligence and hard work. But what does this illusory independence do for one? It enables one to paddle one's own canoe. But that is the illusion: paddling along as the sole occupant of the boat, repelling all boarders and pouring boiling oil on them while pretending that you don't need anyone's help, though you are frantic for it, is the classic neurosis; Scotland is out on a limb; Scotland *needs* England,

Listen to the word of your prophet, who is here to guide you, and who has made his home in the once-happy kingdom that this very dangerous and ruthless woman is sworn to tear asunder, for her own malicious ends. Facing the prospect of our Union's dissolution at the hands of not one, but two, desperately unhappy children, you need to be apprised of the rampant evil skulking below the surface of our conscious mind, unsuspected by all.

*****

There follows an account of the consequences of independence and of the rights associated with it, plus the general background of the Declaration of the Rights of Man and the psychological factors leading to it and resulting from it. Such an account is necessarily far-reaching, and may apparently extend beyond its professed brief; a broadly-based excursion into social contingencies is therefore justified, leading to a greater understanding of the original theme. The crucial subjects of Karma and Samsara also make their appearance, being treated extensively.

Chapter 1

The Iniquity of the Rights of Man; The Cause

'Declaration of Independence', or the Disastrous Fall of Man from Innocence.

The 1776 Declaration of Independence forced on us the notion of the right to rebel in defence of freedom, and a governmental system based on a 'natural law' involving the rights of the individual. Being a pragmatist, and nothing more, I point to this document as the most calamitously devised in history – responsible as it is for war upon war and revolution after revolution. *For it is based on a complete lie: that man has rights*. Quite apart from the fact that no American has ever known what an 'individual' is, no American has even known what a 'right' is, and certainly not what 'freedom' is. In order to obtain 'freedom', one has first to establish whether there is such a thing as freedom and what that freedom consists of.

Individuality, rights and freedom can be lumped together under the dictum, "individuality confers rights and freedom on itself". Therefore, to have any freedom or rights one has first to possess individuality, which is won after a lifetime's battle with oneself, not with one's fellow man, and finally confers the right, and freedom, to think. It is not affected by any outside, or political, agency, and, other than the opportunity to think, there is no right known to man.

Such political 'individuality' as exists is a mere numerative denomination, and, far from being individual, it is in fact profoundly collective and unconscious. Americans are, more than any other race in the civilised world, the least able to think. The only thing they are clever at is making a 'fast buck' – and making an H-Bomb for blowing humanity off the face of the earth.

This manifesto was fostered by the illusion that God himself has endowed man with rights. God never intended man to have any rights whatever – those being regarded as something that we can demand, on the basis that humanity is entitled to hold Creation to ransom. Creation in fact makes it quite clear that, as there are many essential processes in the world, they cannot be usurped by the application of rights to suit man's convenience, and that under no circumstances can evolution's laws be interfered with. Whatever claims man may make upon the powers that be, for the direction of society, *he must realise that this direction is already in place under the charge of evolution itself*. The promotion of the common man over the greater direction of society – already under way – is insupportable and wrong; man-made laws are neither ordained by Nature, nor inalienable, nor self-evident, and they are not in any way binding on whatever higher authority gets in their way.

The Rights of Man are in no way inevitable or obligatory, and cannot be imposed universally or indiscriminately. There are countries in the world who reject these laws precisely because they are imposed without consideration for the very many exceptions to the rule; in fact there are so many exceptions that, in the Asiatic half of the world, the opposite is the natural law. In these countries, the introduction of rights would jeopardise a perfectly viable social system and would be completely disruptive to a differing psychological background.

The idea, implicit – or explicit – in the Declaration, that rights should be applied to everyone and everything right across the board, is in fact a dictation of the very sort that the document was designed to prevent. And in case you think that America couldn't be so unreasonable, just cock an ear to what Bush is declaring and ranting about incessantly.

The peasants were peasants because they had no intelligence; they were not 'born' to their lowly estate. Nor were they 'kept down'; they simply did not have the aptitude to climb up: exactly the situation that the 'Rights of Man' was designed to perpetuate.

The conception of 'freedom', so prized in America, was apparently founded on the belief that everyone in the world, except Americans, was living under tyranny. 'Come to the land of the free'; freedom from what, may I ask? I always understood that Britain herself, from whom the USA sought to part company, so prized her own freedom that she fought against Napoleon – not to mention the Kaiser and then Hitler – to preserve it. Man's freedom may be a desirable thing, but man does not have a right to it, and certainly not the right to demand it. In fact, the 'natural' freedom of man does not even exist, and can never exist; the only freedom granted by God to man, apart from the capacity to think, is to die – and even that is taken away from us by the Hippocratic Oath.

The USA's undying intention is to impose freedom on everyone and everything else, regardless of circumstances and with unlimited powers to dictate its acceptance.

Americans have to take a tumble to themselves, and realise that their nation was founded on a complete chimera. Hard as it may be to believe, and contrary to all viciously-held traditions in America, this fact has to be acknowledged and accepted; otherwise there is no hope for world peace. The United States is the threat, not Russia or China.

There was no justification, of course, for Bin Laden's attack on New York, and America has every right to retaliate, which is why the war in Afghanistan, at least, is a 'just' one. Fundamentalism is an evil that must be expurgated. However, what Bin Laden is fighting against is not the illusion of freedom, but values, held in the Western world, that are inimical to all innocent ideas supporting the lives of decent and self-respecting people everywhere else. Offensive beliefs emanating from Europe and America did in fact provoke the '9/11' disaster. That they also provoked Bin Laden's personal inferiority complex is largely irrelevant, except that this sense of inferiority is widespread throughout the East and results not least from America's arrogance.

There are more wars caused by the actual *idea* of freedom than by any physical necessity for it, such is human susceptibility, and this unsubstantiated belief in the obligatory 'call to arms' has produced more wars since the Declaration of Independence than at any previous time in history. Contrary to the popular belief in the USA that Britain wielded tyrannical power over that fledgling country, the American Revolution was actually caused by the somewhat less significant attempt to impose taxes on the tea industry; apart from that, British rule was not objectionable, and was only thought to be so when George Washington managed to persuade his impressionable countrymen that rule from London was somehow undesirable; and being imbued with the notion that his destiny and that of his country were bound up, he came to the irresistible conclusion that he had been chosen – by someone unspecified – to conduct a crusade against what would normally be considered a rather reasonable regime. But there you are; George never told a lie, did he?

The idea that the United States was preternaturally destined to lead 'the warriors of freedom' in a holy war against all and sundry was both the cause and the result of that country's totally unfounded assumption that God had his eye on the American people. How they knew that, I don't know, because God never told me anything of the sort, and I was under the impression that I was here to prove exactly the opposite. So one of us has to go. I will definitely be crucified – there is no doubt about that – and the Americans are just the buggers to do it; if I dare set foot over there, I am sure Uncle Sam will set the dogs onto me. But that is a risk I have to take; the need to put down America's rampant ego is too important to be abandoned.

The world was not invented for the masses, whose prophet is an elitist. Existence is a gift awarded to those who are prepared to exert themselves, man's chief quality being, unfortunately, laziness. Therefore, an end to all revolutions and the damnable right to life, liberty, and the pursuit of happiness, the last of which can only be found in the service of others and the sacrifice of personal freedom.

American is founded on a lie – nay, a series of lies – and far from being the self-styled saviour of the world, it has been a primary source of world suffering – unwitting to itself, maybe, but thereby all the more to be condemned. I bring consciousness, and there is no greater enemy of man than the abysmal absence of that quality, which is the subliminal cause of the proposed imposition of rights and freedom in the first place. Unless the USA and the rest of the world realise the basic lie at the root of man's condition – there is no hope of anyone attaining any freedom – freedom, that is, from the lie itself. Other than the freedom of the conscious individual to think for himself, there is no freedom, and there was never designed to be any. The only God-given right of man was, indeed, the God-given freedom of the enterprising citizen to meditate of his own volition; that was declared vociferously by Europeans hundreds of years ago, and not latterly by some insolent band of American Fathers.

The lie at the root of man's condition is nothing less than the universal belief that "I am as great as God". That is why man *crucifies* God – because, in spite of himself, he knows the truth and he can't accept it. I bring the truth; I will be crucified.

In declaring man's entitlement to absolute freedom, and his absolute right to this, that and the other, man is setting himself up as God, for only God has the right to make such laws. Democracy, far from being a God-given sentiment, would, more accurately, be from the Devil, for, in its pursuit there have been countless acts of mass violence,

The clown currently at the helm of the Western world was voted in on the basis of his nice smile and the public's willingness to overlook his obvious mental deficiency, these being his sole qualifications. The cowboy in jeans, who should have stayed mucking the pigs out on his ranch, managed to con the West into accepting his version of the USA's perennial manifesto. By a combination of their leader's egoism and their own unassailable naïveté – a distinguishing feature of these people – the citizens of America have been led into one state of confrontation after another, on the platform of the deluded proclamation that man has rights. From that alone there has issued a constant international tension, and the egos, both national and individual (and also the naïveté) of the hostile countries have invariably been inflamed by the illusion that freedom – whatever that is – is obligatory to every self-respecting man; and despite the frightful consequences of fratricidal conflict, brother has turned on brother, and both together have turned on what is more often than not an inoffensive and benign government. Shouting the odds against one and all, these macho heroes take a swipe at anything they suspect of having designs on their manhood – and the alleged oppression by any hapless government is enough to persuade them of that. Freedom in the name of manhood is the creed that inspires, and confuses, most primitive mentalities, which are unable to distinguish between the demands of egoism and a possible intellectual cause. Rousing the rabble is a vested interest of so-called intellectuals the world over, and so much the better if it is based on a lie. This usually results in the confusion of the idea of maleness with the desire to 'throw off the yoke' – a cry that never fails to appeal to the tribal war-mongers, whether or not it is accompanied by a reason. From the jungles of Africa to the more sophisticated ale-houses of Edinburgh, the eternal incitement to take up arms is met with immediate enthusiasm; and even if, as in the case of Edinburgh, the bearing of offensive weapons is not required, Scottish manhood rallies to the cause; "Down with England!

What have those buggers ever done for us? Ever since Robert the Bruce shuffled off this mortal coil, those English fuckers have levied taxes on our whisky and stolen the salt off our porridge!"

Alex Salmond, a stern representative of human rights and freedom – at least, when it comes to Scotland – is particularly clamorous, though I have not, as yet, been able to perceive any objective reasons for his rabid incantations against his historical neighbour. It is a bit out of date, wouldn't you say? Maybe two or three hundred years ago it would have been appropriate to preach fire and brimstone against the English oppressor, but can you tell me exactly how England is oppressing him today?

Despite the civilisation, i.e. the cultural and economic development, that Scotland has derived from the English, and which has rescued it from the hordes of kilted heathens, there has arisen in the misty north a belatedly dissenting voice that is determined to prove how superior in every way Scotland is to England. That this conviction emanates from Salmond's own overweening ego and not directly from that of the average Scottish clansman is a fact yet to be rumbled by the slumbering natives both north and south of the border. The Declaration has worked its invidious influence even amongst the sublimely unconscious peaks and valleys of our once-united Kingdom. The obvious necessity for unity in our troubled world is being deliberately obstructed by the call for liberty and privileges that is broadcast, universally and incessantly, with the aim of inspiring innocent, though gullible, people to rise up against what is misrepresented as 'oppression'. Countries such as Tibet and Burma, which genuinely do suffer from oppression, are in the very exceptional minority, being governed, unfortunately by regimes that exhibit an infantile mentality and are subject to the most primitive beliefs. These nations have every excuse to use violence, but they are counselled in the instance of Tibet, by the wise old Dalai Llama, who forbids violence under any circumstances.

The Dalai Llama also counsels that Tibet should remain, whatever the outcome of the protest, under Chinese rule. This would, of course, provide the ideal solution, *as it would preserve an indispensable unity.* The Chinese may eventually bow to world opinion, *that having been inspired by the unarmed resistance, and peaceful protests of the Tibetans.* What the Tibetans are seeking to achieve *is the freedom of the individual to conduct his own inward-looking meditation; in other words, freedom to think.* This is the 'religion' that the Chinese are trying to suppress; *in a totalitarian state, a free-thinking individual poses a threat: he questions its authority.*

And so it is, in the apparently free world of the West. We in the West use exactly the same tactics as the Chinese, to the same end; any society founded on the right of the establishment to impose the very suppression it is ostensibly designed to prevent is in danger of succumbing to schizophrenia. The only way to save such a society is to introduce *freedom: the freedom of the individual to think*. In the absence of thinking, society goes under.

America is as much the enemy as China (or Iran). Freedom is threatened by China on a physical basis, but America threatens the very freedom she professes to defend; man has only one freedom and that is to think for himself, and it is this, precisely, that America is attacking.

It is not only America's own ego that sparked off the '9/11' attack, but also the very aggression demonstrated by the US in her 'declaration of intent'. This is a direct challenge to the ego, and obviously to the freedom as well, of other countries. What we have here is the *confrontation of egos, and the mutual threat to freedom. This is the classic cause of all wars,*

It is probably true that China threatens America on a purely *physical* basis, and that America threatens China on a *mental* basis, since neither nation can actually think (as far as politicians are concerned) and such intellectual freedom as they both have is extrovert on America's part and introvert on China's, these two psychological functions actually being the even more fundamental cause of the conflict, representing, as they do, the intellectual *character* of each party. On the one hand we have the individual nature of the Chinese mentality; on the other we have the collective nature of America's; *this has always been the underlying, and even more basic, source of antagonism, throughout world history.*

The only way this constant threat to world peace can be overcome *is by the conscious address of both the egoistic and the psychological differences, while the actual identity of the two modes of thinking must be acknowledged.*

Because China's psyche is basically introverted, her thinking function (confined to her intellectuals) *is conscious and therefore far more individual than America's.* America's psyche being basically extroverted, her thinking function is *unconscious and therefore essentially collective.* Because thinking, in China, is *conscious* and, in America, *unconscious*, it follows that China's psyche is not only individual but also comparatively free, while America's is collective and therefore captive. Therefore America is defending her freedom – a purely physical devotion to a numerical individuality – *against a physical attack, while China feels her freedom threatened mentally;* of the two, China's mental attitude is by far the more intelligent, and consequently America should seriously consider whether her freedom is actually as valuable as her enemy's: the freedom to do no more than eat, sleep and fart – the habitual American programme – can hardly be compared to Asia's free application of metaphysics.

The difference between the two egos is apportioned on a similar basis. We have, on the one hand, the introverted inferiority complex of Asia and, on the other, the extroverted superiority complex of the West. They complement each other: the schizophrenic division between the world's hemispheres, neither being aware of the other's true nature, each tearing the other's throat out as a consequence. As far as egoism is concerned, both are equally culpable, China's initial inferiority giving rise to her desire for superiority – in all things, from territorial conquest to possession of the atom bomb – America's *resultant* superiority ensuing from her *initial* inferiority – that arising from the occidental self-comparison with God himself, purely unconsciously. These are facts that can very easily be proved, being the underlying reality: man is a primitive and savage beast.

The intellectual life of China is, or was before Mao Tse Tung, far more advanced than that of the US, and also on a far wider scale, being present particularly in Buddhist monasteries, Buddhism being as much a philosophy as a religion; in comparison, America's intellect is non-existent. Peace is founded on negotiation, not on the threat to drop bombs on everyone who opposes you. It is this very threat, carried out by the USA not only in the past but also right now, that was largely responsible for the war in Iraq, for which there proved to be no reason, never mind an excuse, except for America's customary bellicosity and bloody-mindedness, in which a minimum of diplomacy disguises the underlying desire to solve everything by force.

Bush and Blair were itching to flex their muscle – what leader wouldn't? – and despite the predictable denial, this was the unconscious and ultimate purpose of their being in power: to save the country by flattening any aggressor; what are all those planes and ships waiting for? Go on! This is the ultimate test of your manhood! Push the button!

In anticipation of the fury of apologists, I repeat that this is the *unconscious,* or *subliminal,* purpose of being a leader; look to the psyche within.

The annihilation of Iraq was brought about by the monstrous ego of America, and that of Mr Blair, which persuaded them, against the promptings of reality, to bomb the bloody shit out of the place. Despite Blair's assumption that he is a reasonable and peaceful man, this restrained attitude did not prevent him, without needing much persuasion, from unleashing the holocaust, Saddam's personal proclivities being dragged in afterwards as an excuse.

How, by any stretch of the imagination, could Saddam possibly have attacked either England or America in their homelands? And if this whole campaign was conducted on the basis that we were stepping in to pre-empt a possible conflict somewhere in the Middle East (a comparatively restricted area, and not on our own doorstep), another professed motive – why would we need to get our knickers in a twist over that? The 'World Policeman' retired long ago; NATO wouldn't take a hand for the same reason.

The American military, of course, could not wait to go into action to show those cowardly Iraqis just how brave and tough the American 'fighting man' is, and that is the sole motive for the American soldier's decision to join the army – to prove to the world that he is 'top dog' and that everyone else is a quaking poltroon, as demonstrated in every war film and best-seller, and shouted to the rooftops by the nation's own habitual attitude – frayed at the edges latterly but still persistent – bristling with aggression and mean intent. The truth, as usual, will be brushed aside because ego itself blinds us to it.

The whole creed on which the American nation was founded, and its subsequent traumatizing effect on the rest of the planet, was based on a criminal misrepresentation, and this fact, which will be angrily rejected, has led to the belief on the part of its citizens that that country was set up by God to represent man's right to absolute freedom; and in defence of their own entitlement to this illusory quality, they are prepared to plunge the world into even deeper chaos, as we have seen in Iraq and, furthermore, in the USA's declared intention to reduce Iran too to rubble.

There was in fact no negotiation between the Allies and Saddam, beyond ultimatums; such sanctions as there were had been put in place long before to topple a repressive regime, and this idea was only trotted out as the excuse for the invasion when it was discovered belatedly that there were no weapons of mass destruction after all. Having his justification taken away from him, what did Blair do but play the card of 'regime-change', when, previously, it had not 'figured'? No doubt convincing even himself, Blair managed to fudge the issue so that a not too observant public was also convinced. The 'toppling of the tyrant' became the government's very popular order of the day; amongst all the furore, who now remembers 'weapons of mass destruction'?

A pre-emptive strike in order to protect Cyprus against rockets that did not have nuclear warheads was, therefore, hardly justified, while the defence of Kuwaiti oilfields might actually have *had* justification, given that force is regarded as the only solution in a militaristic world. The protection of Cyprus and Kuwait would not have necessitated, and fortunately did not lead to, an invasion of the offending country.

Unless we are to assume that the whole war was conducted in defence of Israel (which wouldn't surprise me), where the rockets, purportedly, could also reach, we are faced with the inescapable conclusion that Blair, at least, is guilty of mass deception, the failure to acknowledge the Israeli factor having been another dishonest omission. Such an acknowledgement might, of course, have plunged us into a war with the whole Arab world, so perhaps self-preservation may excuse mendaciousness?

The absolute refusal of the United States to even consider that its core belief could be wrong presents the world with an insoluble problem; not only are the Western leaders subject to schizophrenia – that particular psychosis being partly a schism between truth and reality, exacerbated by general contradictions and inconsistencies – but they are also incapable of thinking rationally, which is actually consistent with the illness. But on no account would Blair admit this; Bush might, because his naïve mentality leaves him open to the persuasion that "all good men admit their faults".

But between the two of them they manage to present a united front, thus lending stability to an otherwise unstable mental condition; If you are convinced that you are a messiah – another thing Blair professes unconsciously – you might very well decide to dispense with all reason and substitute your gut-feelings in every way possible; and because Blair is a quasi-Communist – when it suits him – nevertheless managing to conduct an illicit affair with Conservatism, his gut feelings tell him to fool the world into thinking he is both. This, of course, is impossible, because, as we know, Labour and Conservative would never be seen in bed together; but in Blair's mind there is no distinction between Red and Blue, and also no distinction between truth and falsehood.

In accord with the convolutions of the schizophrenic mentality, Blair's situation is understandable; on the one hand he convinces himself that he is Red, on the other hand he convinces himself that he is Blue; but where he falls down is in trying to convince himself, also, that he is *both at the same time*. Not even a schizophrenic can do that. The pathological mind is polarized; in other words, you can't have your cake and eat it at the same time. The trouble with Blair is that he doesn't know whether he's got his cake in the first place, or how to bloody well eat it anyway.

So it should be evident by now that our Prime Minister is in no position to pass judgement on world affairs.

*****

Once the Americans had scented blood, nothing could stop them. What in fact scented blood was not so much their noses as their insane egos. *Ego is a fact, and never more so than in America; it drives the economy, it drives the government, it drives the psyche.* This nation, boasting to be the champion of the free world, is so governed by egoism that it cannot see its own infamy; and rather than admit what to everyone else is the screamingly obvious truth, it sends envoys around the world charged with persuading everyone that this belligerent hive of conceit is their best friend; read it in America's eyes, read it in America's face, read it in America's brutally arrogant behaviour – which it doesn't even attempt to disguise, so convinced is it that God is on its side.

This must be said; this must be believed; otherwise the USA. will continue to trample on all who get in her way. Her self-belief is *beyond* belief; her blindness to herself is only surpassed by her blindness to others.

The original Declaration was inspired by the unfounded conception of 'God's Own Country' –

notwithstanding that identical assumption on the part of other nations. All this was compounded by the ego of the average citizen, which was in turn fostered by a rather mysterious thing, in far-off Europe, called the 'Social Contract'. Whatever the original meaning, or purpose, of this contract, it took root in the USA more than any other country, as the subliminal relationship between the ego of the private citizen and the even more overwhelming ego of the nation as a whole – represented, of course, by the 'American Fathers' themselves. All the egoistic strands of this relationship – that is, the individual citizens – were held together and facilitated by what I have described as 'the collective confidence trick' – a process of mutual blackmail: "You scratch my back and I'll scratch yours – but woe betide you if you don't". Present in most countries of the world, the mutual confidence trick is, and was at that time, modified by the very process it entails; for, in its intention to subdue all genuinely 'individual' resistance, it actually consolidates and draws together the membership of society as a whole, so providing it with an essential unity - its original purpose. *The fabric of civilisation is therefore based on its own warp and woof: the intricate interweaving, and interlocking, of its many egoistic parts.*

Individual resistance obviously has to be suppressed because, by thinking, the individual sees the gaping flaws in society's structure – and in those days he was burnt at the stake for doing so. However, the diabolical process of suppression, carried out by society against itself, takes place nowadays on a more insidious basis; but, put in a nutshell, it would proceed like this; "You keep my ego going, and I'll keep yours going, and together we'll keep society's going". And let me tell you that there is nothing more truly diabolical than Egoic Man – both towards himself, unwittingly, and towards others.

Chapter 2

The Infamous Declaration

The only right man has is to become himself through thinking. He certainly has no right to assert himself, and still less right to expect *any* rights. God put us on earth for his own purposes, meaning that we are here on sufferance; we are God's retainers, and retainers have no rights except to be retained. God's dispensation cannot be thrown back in his face by a demonstration of tantrums, designed to compel him to withdraw his intentions.

The most destructive event of modern times was America's misconceived Declaration of sundry rights; this unfortunate occurrence has had the most dire consequences for mankind ever since, causing endless war and presenting us, on the home front, with women's rights and the feminist movement – all having the one intention of defying God's purpose for man, which is to have no rights at all. In defying God's most basic law, America has introduced chaos onto earth, which we see constantly around us in the demands, on every possible occasion and against all reason, for 'life, liberty, and the pursuit of happiness'. Happiness will never be found in the arms of either life or liberty; life, or existence, is demonstrably an illusion, and liberty has yet to be proved desirable. The assumption that any of these three qualities is either necessary *or* desirable is unwarranted and has never been substantiated. Far to the contrary, our subsequent history has proved exactly the opposite. The world would not be in the mess we see today if Thomas Jefferson had not been drunk on the Fourth of July; only a befuddled mind could have produced such a fallacious idea. His intellectual qualifications were not inspiring, consisting of an over-zealous knowledge of the Bible and a few philosophical persuasions culled from other peoples' concepts – and not much else. Along with a few other unqualified pundits he has managed to convince the 'free' world that freedom – if there actually is such a thing – is worth fighting for, indeed, that it is obligatory to fight for it. First of all, the true nature of freedom has never been revealed to the world – I am bringing it for the first time – and, secondly, it is doubtful that two catastrophic world wars have actually proved that fifty million dead mean it was worth it. That the 'free world' remains is due not so much to the fighting capacities of the American soldier as to the fact that the few hundred million survivors managed to avoid extinction.

Freedom, therefore, as defined by Thomas Jefferson, has proved to cause more misery and suffering than it was reputed to prevent. Is it actually worth fighting for? I like fighting, myself, but I have yet to meet the grieving mother who thought the sacrifice of her son was worth the blood and gore that produced it. The American soldier's attempt to prove how heroic he is – constantly thrust in our faces by John Wayne – is the underlying force behind his country's persistent determination to go to war. This all-consuming desire for heroism and sacrifice, in the alleged service of an illusory freedom, stems from the same disastrous romantic fantasy that produced the 'Declaration' in the first place.

*****

Western culture has developed an obsession with personal freedom. This very obsession has produced exactly the opposite result to its intended aim: *it has ended personal freedom. Every Western society is now a totalitarian state.* That is not an exaggeration; it is not an extreme statement. I wish it were.

You, the Western citizen, have turned yourself inside out; black has become white, white has become black, *Good has become evil: exaggerated good automatically becomes its opposite.* And, in this case, the desire to introduce personal freedom *has become* exaggerated; safeguards to personal freedom have been removed, the chief of them being the ability to think. No one can think if he is denied the facility to do so; that is, a thinking environment, or an environment conducive to thinking. When Tony Blair took it upon himself to abolish the grammar schools – evidently to disguise the source of his own education, public schools being only one step removed – he destroyed the primary access of the working classes to intellectual distinction. This hypocritical attempt to do away with his past – in fact to betray his own origins for cheap popularity – was designed to prove to working folk that he was 'one of them'. And what better could you have than that? Betray your own heritage, and the world is yours.

But in attempting to prove this to the working man, Blair in fact removed the very source of the working man's education. By the admission of the majority, grammar schools had provided the best, and only, route to success. And now where are they? They have been replaced by all sorts of queer establishments, culminating in something called an 'academy'; which, as far as I can make out, are actually no different, except in name, from the original grammar schools. They serve exactly the same purpose – which is, if I am not mistaken, 'higher education' (or is it 'further education'?) But of course, the original purpose of abolishing grammar schools, apart from Blair's personal disavowal, was to deprive the working man of 'higher education' – otherwise, why abolish them? The other purpose, naturally, was to poke the intelligent members of working society in the eye, and prevent them succeeding. Now, the working man, paradoxically, has been got in by the back door – courtesy of the academies – so that we won't know he is receiving higher education - or so I must assume, because by now I am beginning to realise that the Labour Party, as well as being deceitful, must be schizophrenic. If you can figure out the desperate convolutions, contradictions, withdrawals and reinstatements sent, evidently, to reduce the educational system to chaos, you are a better man than I am – and I shall retire to a rest home.

But the secret is out. Don't I hear you telling me that the real reason grammar schools were abolished was the intention *to make everybody equal?* Well, I am sorry to inform you that no one on earth can make everyone else on earth equal; that is God's job, and he says that under no circumstances *should* everyone be equal – that in fact it is *impossible* for everyone to be equal. Are you as clever as I am? And if you are not, then you are not entitled, by any natural law, to be educated to a higher level; you are simply not intelligent enough; the teachers would be wasting their time, and if by some fluke you ended up in a decent job, you would very soon be sacked. The world is for the intelligent: God says so, and, by all the laws of evolution, the success of this planet is based on 'the survival of the fittest' - not just when the monkeys were playing around, but also now that the contest is between minds. I could take two of you on and reduce you to mincemeat – which is why I have been selected by Nature to write this sermon.

This prophet, sent to instruct the universe, is an elitist – and proud of it. Furthermore, he is a Conservative, and would have no truck with Labourites, or any other trogs, if he could possibly avoid it. Labour is based on 'equality for all', and even if you take that to mean 'equal opportunities', the whole idea is scuppered from the start by the inability of the common man to muster the intelligence for it. Equal opportunities are wasted opportunities, and if Labour insists on promoting the herd, let it not do so at the expense of those who are clever enough, and sufficiently motivated, to make their own way in the world; that means not holding them back, in schools and classes that are designed specifically for the mentally deficient. Unfortunately, three-quarters of the population *is* mentally-deficient, thus rendering it necessary to reinstate the grammar schools.

Chapter 3

The Result

How democracy is a front for man's self-deception

Attention, all public relations wallahs! Established as you are at the heart of public affairs, you must be aware that a more dishonourable occupation never slithered across the face of society. Teaching your clients how to twist their neighbours, how to employ every dirty trick in the book, how to lie without being found out – this is how you proceed, despite your undoubted ability to remain oblivious to it. All this is calculated, and disguised so as to be acceptable to the more gullible of us, notwithstanding your efforts to present an innocent face, which is quite deliberate, though, of course, unconscious.

The prime example of this regime of deceit, but by no means the exception to it whether against society or, more to the point, against one's self, is Max Clifford, late advisor to the rich and famous.

The most degrading profession ever to disgrace the office of business, or any other office, features as its cornerstone an invidious school of charm which teaches one to dissemble without alerting the victim, and arms one with the confidence to cheat without the inconvenience of guilt – the modern trend being to approach life from the point of view of total cynicism, no genuine feelings being allowed in this world of sophistication, where any suggestion of innocence is dismissed as immature and wet. This, of course, doesn't matter, because everyone in society subscribes to the assumption that life is a charade and that therefore we are entitled – even obliged – to conduct ourselves on a spurious and shallow basis. The more people we dupe, the more sophisticated we are considered to be. This is the unspoken and underlying reality of contemporary psychology.

The cultivation of deliberate artifice is now expressly taught in our universities and in schools of 'self-development', the latter having mushroomed ever since the Hollywood Attitude displaced the common sense of our more impressionable citizens. And if you don't recognize this as yourself, your capacity for self-deception equals your capacity for deceiving others.

Such are the credentials of the brigade of public relations officers lately recruited into politics, as the advisory experts in the background; these advisors have reduced the government to a body of shysters intent on misleading the country at every turn of their mendacious mentalities. Exaggerated, you say; here again, if you don't believe what I am saying, you should take a closer look at yourself – under that calculated front. The smug, angelic, self-satisfied smiles of the Labour front-bench spokeswomen say everything that needs to be said about the true face of the cabinet. Their holier-than-thou, sanctimonious assumption that they, and only they, are right – on every question – and could not be otherwise, sickens all those with an objective viewpoint. You may not think that it bears particular significance, but let me assure you that this very assumption of theirs belies their apparent innocence – an innocence that is actually the most destructive and deceptive part of their make-up; for it is deliberately intended to disguise the iron fist in the velvet glove. These very attractive women, in whose mouths butter wouldn't melt, are in reality the hellions behind Labour's collective ego – and ego, let me add, supersedes even deceptive innocence as the most destructive part of their psychology, being the very thing that innocence is at such pains to conceal. Who said women don't have egos? Particularly women in high places.

Their evident belief that the Labour party is uniquely destined to lead the world into the promised land of purity and plenty, where everyone would worship their political leaders as messiahs, is somewhat contradicted by the unfortunate truth: that Labour's pristine virtue is sullied by the illusion that divine right confers on them an exemption from all criticism – which they normally and habitually dismiss with a wave of their intolerant hand. They will deny this with every breath; they wouldn't want to think that their dainty little hands would tamper with the process of truth – such delicate, lady-like behaviour as they exhibit in the service of the welfare state could not possibly be contaminated by *un*-ladylike egotism – the snake that lurks just beneath the surface of our so-placid lives.

The grey iniquity of the next incumbent prime minister, Brown himself, may be unwitting, but it is all the more redolent of Lucifer for that; the more inoffensive and plausible we seem, you may be sure that we are the opposite underneath, the character of the primitive savage having remained unsubdued since primeval history – leading us into predatory behaviour even in the sacrosanct quarters of politics.

While maintaining his Presbyterian façade, Brown subliminally pursues a dangerous course of misrepresentation, designed to convince everyone that he is, on the one hand, the Angel Gabriel – doing as his father demanded while he was a callow youth – and, on the other hand, that he and his ministers have nothing but the people at heart; whereas the fact is that they are occupied in milking the susceptibilities of a vulnerable electorate, to the extent of persuading them that everything in the Labour government's policies is not only hunky-dory but actually beyond any possibility of contradiction, and that their self-projected image is sacrosanct – "and we dare you to question that". There is none so blind as man to himself.

Incredible! Unacceptable! You cry. But look at you: are you in any position to judge? - You, who are so unaware of your own proclivities that you believe *yourself* to be sacrosanct? Beyond reproach, even? So you are convinced when treading the corridors of power.

Where, actually, does the truth lie? The average politician, bereft as he is of the refinements of conscious living, is immersed, as we have said, in ego, unable to think in even the simplest terms – beyond the calculation of the daily bowel movement – and so unconscious as not to know anything of significance; possessing, furthermore, so little will that his mind bows to the slightest mental pressure. This unfortunate automaton struts around Westminster as if he had the right to be there, which indeed he wouldn't have if his true mental capacity were suspected. He furthermore exhibits the characteristics of a quivering jelly in the face of physical attack; rather than hit somebody in retaliation, he would actually resort to suing them in court. And he leads our country?

All in all, we are represented by a gang of self-serving opportunists – in contrast to their own, self-deluding belief. This is a portrait of the human being: if you do not recognize yourself, take heart from the monkey's inability to reflect on anything at all.

What do I think of Blair? A public relations expert, only surpassed in that regard by Alastair Campbell, the author of 'New Labour' – a scheme as dishonest as its creator – which was designed to manipulate the public into accepting a few adventurers as the leaders of our country, with as few political qualifications as possible; and, further, to maintain them in power as long as they succeed in hoodwinking parliament with diabolically clever speeches – learned from years of wheeling and dealing at the Bar. The 1997 election was fought and won on the grounds of scurrilous allegations by New Labour – dug up by nocturnal investigations into the parliamentary dunghill – against those unfortunate members of the Tory Party who had dared to indulge in extramarital affairs –

which would not have excited a murmur if Blair and his cohorts had not been determined to drive them out, by fair means or foul. All fair politics? Not in the hands of past masters of smear and calumny campaigns. Yes, Tony, this is how you came to power; *you* may have forgotten it, but *I* haven't. You have, as usual, pushed it underground, in favour of that sickly niceness you know so well how to project. And don't maintain that Labour won the election on the strength of its policies; the gullible public was persuaded, by such policies as were advanced, that they, the Labour rank and file, were entitled to anything they wanted – it was theirs by right, they had only to demand it. This, apparently, is democracy: demand and supply. And Labour supplies it. Amongst its bountifulness is the promise that, if the working man does as little as possible, he will be rewarded with the maximum; this has become the unspoken but inalienable law. Complicit in this contract are politicians, intellectuals and social activists alike, plus of course the working man himself. The Social Contract has it that man was put on earth to enjoy as much as possible without actually earning it – an idea inherited from Marxism – and that as a consequence the government was in place to provide free handouts to all you lazy buggers who have been determined since birth to do nothing. Milking the sacred cow of Human Rights is officially encouraged by the Welfare State, which is here to cater for all our needs; If you get VD, pop along to the local hospital and they will cut your chopper off free of charge; the obligation to pay for it doesn't arise, because the working man is not expected to earn enough to make a contribution to anything but the beer he drinks – and he can usually find the money for that. The working classes – represented by 'Joe' – are not expected to earn much because they are not qualified; and they are not qualified because, as we have seen, they have been determined since birth to do nothing. The Welfare State is therefore necessary.

Having decided to do nothing to justify his existence, Joe is encouraged in his idleness by the generosity of the State, which relieves him of the necessity to work and, at the same time, of any guilt he might improbably feel. Marx, and a few psychiatrists, tell us that it is wrong to feel guilty, about anything, because it makes us unhappy; and as a result those whom we have harmed go unsuccoured and unapologised to; which I suppose doesn't matter if Joe carries on oblivious to it, relieved of anything resembling conscience. The Welfare State is therefore designed for the happiness of all of us – particularly those at the bottom, like Joe.

What the State doesn't realise is that Joe isn't entitled, by any natural law, to anything but the socks he stands up in. Somehow Marx, and the psychiatrists he has inspired, have convinced the State that, contrary to expectation, God no longer exists; what God did before he died is either unspecified or hastily forgotten, and I, personally, am unaware of any reason why he would have taken it upon himself to die in the first place. However, I do know that when God *was* alive, he whispered in the ear of those few intelligent enough to take it in that *man is entitled to nothing*. And ever since, in the minds of these intelligent few, this fundamental fact has been preserved. But in the minds of the unintelligentsia, where nothing much but straw resides, a World Plan has been drawn up; and under this Plan, the idea has somehow come about that God, when he was alive, *was a liar*; that he deliberately told us the untruth that man was never destined to have any rights whatever – contrary to the frenzied protestations of every civil rights worker. But God foresaw – presumably before his death – that a plague of civil rights workers would infest the earth, bringing about the destruction of all those natural, and divine, laws that were designed to guide and sustain us through evolution.

Because of this, evolution has come to an end; we are stuck in an impasse between truth and untruth, the truth being that individuality is the Law, and the untruth being that *the world is designed for the common man*. The common man will never become an individual; he is too stupid, he is too indolent; he will never bestir himself. He nevertheless demands that everything should come to him; and the Welfare State, of course, *gives* it to him.

Civilisation was intended for the individual; it thrives on individuality, which contributes to the welfare of the whole by energy and intelligence, and, by self-motivation and self-betterment, fulfils the purpose of evolution. But behold! What do we have? We have a society ruled by the Plan, which dictates that no one need do anything, that certainly no one should be forced to do anything (not even if the fate of the universe depended on it) and that, if the world, in view of this, is to continue, then God from beyond the grave, presumably – is to provide; or, alternatively, the prime minister.

The Plan, of course, is designed by man for the express benefit of that lazy bugger, Joe, of whom, unfortunately, there are so many that they make up the bulk of society, and when those troglodytes work up the energy to vote, is it any wonder that the Conservatives never get in? So trammelled are we by Joe and his mates that the whole social and governmental system is weighed down by a bureaucracy employed entirely for their ends; far from being a society run by individuals, it is answerable fundamentally to a population of useless layabouts, who call the tune. And if you doubt this, take a look at the vociferous majority before you; the common man, accounting for three-quarters of the population, is so mentally inferior – and no amount of education would have altered that – that he has neither the wits nor the determination, nor even any intention, of dragging himself out of his miserable condition. This, if he had the will he could do, like the other quarter who have actually exerted themselves. No, he has not been 'kept down'; his own fecklessness has kept him from rising. How is it that the rest of the citizenry has bettered itself? Rather than put himself to any trouble, like going to a technical college or undertaking an apprenticeship, he prefers to seek the approval of his mates, who, under no circumstances, would exert themselves, and who, abiding by this resolution, impose their will on the weaker members of the fraternity.

So, weak-willed and under the thumb of his associates, our hero proceeds through life like a piece of flotsam adrift on the tide of fate – blaming everyone else for his plight, as he has been instructed to do by all those authorities from Marx onwards, particularly the nanny state, which was set up specifically to confirm and perpetuate this belief. And, ever since, civil rights and social justice have ruled the roost, imposing their will on all and everyone; woe betide anyone who gets in their way!

A Final Note

Two further illusions advance themselves. First, the

disgraceful illusion that there is any genuine poverty in this country – apart from the disgraceful poverty of the pensioners. What poverty is there, may I ask? Everybody has a television, a mobile phone – and probably a computer – a roof over his head, and a square meal at least once a day; no one goes around barefoot, all the kids have pocket-money (a thing that I never had) and the plea that some people are 'homeless' and sleeping on the streets is patent nonsense except in the case of a tramp; anyone without a bed and a roof over his head, including the tramp, *is so by choice*. Strangely enough, they like it; but they will deny that when interviewed in a solicitous fashion. Let there be no doubt about it. The council, in its weakness, provides for all: hostels (which are never full) bed-and-breakfasts, bed-sitters, homes for down and outs. Money to pay for accommodation is no problem, being doled out by the DSS – housing benefit included. Whence come these lies?

The few unfortunate exceptions will have to survive on one meal per day, wrapping themselves in pullovers, coats and blankets if it is cold, until their luck changes – or until they *make* it change. Go to Russia and China to see poverty; "poverty is relative", you say; wealth is also relative.

Second, the David Davies farce. I used to think Davies was intelligent, but he has let himself down by asserting that civil liberties should take precedence over national security; "our freedom is being eroded by further and further laws", he complains. Well let *me* complain that if we did not have the maximum security measures, *we wouldn't have any freedom in the first place, because Al-Quaeda would be bombing us into oblivion*. And if the police are asking for more time to question their suspects, obviously they *need* more time – otherwise they wouldn't be asking for it; and how does David Cameron know how long it takes to question a suspect? The nanny state has been caught with her bloomers down again.

I do not mean to impugn the positive side of Blair – he has done a lot of good for the country, and his concern for public welfare is genuine – *but this is a veneer;* as with all human beings, his positive exterior is belied by a devilish interior. Outwardly his career has been marked by distinct success – a success that disguises a very, very ambitious and ruthless determination. For years, Blair's positive exterior fooled me into thinking that he was a very nice chap, but, at the same time, I had the nagging feeling that all was not right; such a pleasant impression could not possibly tally with his past, nor with the reality I knew very well lay hidden behind that mask; persona and truth have always been subject to the chaotic relationship of Jekyll and Hyde – which affects all of us.

Blair is so concerned with projecting his image of

niceness, that even he himself would never believe the actual truth. He looks very nice, doesn't he, smiling and smirking with complacency as he downs yet another Tory adversary with that calculated perversion of the poor fellow's argument; under that schoolboy's grin lies the insatiable heart of unquenched Ego.

In modern civilisation, the surface show of positivity – and I admit it is positive – is actually a calamitous illusion; under it lies the Primordial Beast, untamed since the beginning of so-called 'evolution': in fact life, *or the progress towards civilisation,* has never achieved its intended goal, humanity having failed miserably to embrace its obligations to itself. The positivity we exhibit is the only evidence of civilisation, the underlying ninety-nine per cent of reality being repressed, partly out of necessity but largely because of our downright ineptitude – a fecklessness common to *all* men.

This is the reality behind all human beings: downright hatred, absolute egotism, *murderous intent,* and total savagery – all concealed from us by rank self-deception. In the depths of the unconscious, we see our true selves – the instinctive, treacherous, constant belligerence between each other and against ourselves; the oh-so-nice exterior, the socially acceptable persona, is a complete blind, set up to hide these very facts. Unfortunately, evolution demands it, from a society that does, when all is said and done, have to defend itself *against* itself. This has to be faced.

Which is the greater truth: the one percent of niceness, affecting us all, or the ninety-nine percent of wickedness, also affecting us all? To which do we address ourselves, with a view to self-correction?

The Declaration of Independence paradoxically indicates, in outwardly cultured form, man's bestiality to man – being prompted by his own conscience, perhaps? But despite his conscience, man's defining factor, driving his politics in particular, is his unconscious atavism, projected in the accepted guise of morality and sententious, high-sounding declarations; all of which demands extirpation. We must grasp our internal evil and convert this raw material into our own self-redemption; for the Divine Spirit will aid us in our efforts, working for us and within us. God does not despair of his errant creatures; for, if it ain't broke, it can't be mended.

Part II

The second part of this book offers instruction on how to attain the only possible kind of independence or freedom.

Chapter 4

Escape from Karma: the One and Only Freedom

In this chapter the Prophet sets out the path
to truth and independence.

There is no such thing as an accident, in so far as it has a cause and a result; that is to say, nothing happens *without* a cause and a result, and so on throughout the chain of existence: this happens because that happened, that happened because something previously happened, stretching right back to infinity, and, because *this* happened, something else *will* happen in the future, all the way *forward* to infinity; *and at infinity they meet, having described a circle.* Beginning meets End, End meets Beginning.

Likewise the chain of desire. Because I desire *that*, that *is* desired, and, because that *is* desired, it desires *that*, which *is* desired and in turn *desires*; so on to infinity, where it eventually *consumes its object*, Beginning meeting End, End meeting Beginning; whereupon the whole process starts again, just as in the chain of existence.

But *does* it start again? What actually happens when desire consumes its object? *The subject of desire, I, consumes the object of desire, you*. The ultimate greed, lust itself, ends up by *devouring* the sexual object: *I devour you*. Surely not a desirable result?

How do we *break* the chain of desire? How do we *stop* it continuing? In devouring its object, desire *extinguishes* its object; and because there is nothing left to desire, desire itself dies; life becomes extinct.

Therefore remove the object; deprive the object of its power to attract desire - by making it vanish.

How can *I* make *you*, the object of desire, vanish? How can I, the desiring subject, make you, the desired object, disappear?

Somehow the answer must be found in the Eternal Paradox: the simultaneous and reciprocal relationship of subject and object. *While I desire you, you are desired by me, and while you are desired by me, you desire me*. But the object is not *you; you are a spirit, a being. Therefore, if I desire a spirit, and the spirit is desired by me, both I and the spiritual object of desire have entered the realm of Spirit.* In the realm of Spirit anything can happen, anything is possible; *for it lies outside the physical world, which is governed by its own restriction, or limitation, to itself. It cannot see, or reach, beyond itself, being limited to its own disciplines and its own self-perpetuating character of cause and effect or life and death.*

The eternal wheel of life and death, and the eternal wheel of desire, are bound up in the eternal round, or chain, of existence: Samsara.

Therefore, step outside Samsara. And the only way to step outside anything, including one's own physical existence, is by consciousness. Consciousness would not mean much if it merely led, as in Buddhist belief, to freedom through dissolution of the self; instead, what Neo-Christianity proposes is that freedom should be sought by *reconciliation* of the self with physical existence; that is, freedom should be sought *within* existence. Thus time and timeless would be brought to a rapprochement in the Eternal Present, which does not truly exist in Buddhism; the Buddhist might witness the Eternal, but it is the Eternal without time, or existence. The Eternal Present must be realised *here and now,* in the immediacy of the Neo-Christian version of Nirvana, within the material world.

The Kingdom of Heaven, or Eternity, would, as

predicted so often in the Bible, *be established on earth.* Unfortunately, most of Christ's teaching was either not recorded or deliberately obscured, but whichever it was, it has been lost to posterity; I, as a modern Christian prophet, can only surmise its substance.

Take half an ounce of Karma and half an ounce of Eternity, mix, and you might end up with the Eternal Present, in which cause and effect, in common with the subject and object of desire, are *severed* from each other by the Universal Schism, which was sent for no other purpose than to separate. Cause and effect is perpetual because it belongs to the state of Unity; that is, the state of Collectivity that governs the Asiatic world. Collectivity, or Unity, is the breeding-ground of cause and effect, from which the Asian has no hope of breaking free except by Buddhist teaching; but, as we have seen, that teaching does not restore the adept to the world of existence that he has left behind; nor does it free him from Unity. The adept will find freedom from Unity in separation, or duality, a concept that Buddhism abhors; the Opposites, let us say subject and object or cause and effect, have achieved separation in the West through the Fall of Man, by which the Universal schism was introduced to existence. Consciousness was, at the same time, and as a direct result, created; so, in the West, began man's paradoxical love-hate relationship with the two halves of his psyche – consciousness and unconsciousness. Although they are designed to serve in partnership, the former has always been determined to displace, if not annihilate, the latter.

We cannot consider the conscious mind without the unconscious mind; indeed, in accepting their partnership, we have the basis for the resolution of life's deepest problems, just as in accepting the fundamental duality, or paradox, of existence, something that the Buddhist would never do. To solve the problem of karma, or samsara, *in the Eternal Present of existence*, rather than in a far off and inaccessible Eternity, we need, simultaneously, to separate and unite, or re-unite, subject and object, cause and effect.

First, drive a wedge between the two opposites, nullifying their relationship and thereby withdrawing their power over each other; in doing so, we at once disarm desire – or, at least, deprive it of its successful expression. Desire is now stuck, frustratedly, in between subject and object.

But desire consists of will: I desire You. If I *desire* You, I can *un*-desire You, by reversing my will. Everyone, however, is subject to desire, and the only way to overcome it is by Love: devote your will to Love – tuck it under Love's wing, where you will find enough relief from desire to suit any human. But if you are a god, or if you *must* be a god, you will not be satisfied by this solution; only an all-out attack on will would suffice.

There are two wills: the Collective, or One, Will and the Individual Will; they fight like hell – murderously, in fact; neither will rest until it has annihilated the other. But as far as the average human is concerned, the Collective Will is bound to win.

However, be aware of paradox, for in this contest of wills, it is imperative that the ordinary individual should challenge the One, or Collective, Will, *which resides within the individual himself*. Therefore, frustrate what is in effect your own will, by suppressing it though not repressing it; the two wills are conflated, both reacting very strongly to this attack. By such means you will *strengthen and develop* your will, for *it is at once that which is suppressed and that which is doing the suppression*.

At the same time as the development of your will, the development of your consciousness will take place, the one resulting in the other. By the suppression of your will, I do of course mean *your will to desire*, desire itself undergoing frustration.

In frustrating, or mastering, desire, we use the twin instruments of will and consciousness, amalgamated as *conscious-will;* consciousness guides the will, will implements consciousness.

The adept travelling the road to enlightenment, or freedom, hopes eventually to become the conscious being who has achieved Nirvana, or the state of freedom itself. But the average adept, who probably wouldn't become a conscious being, or minor Buddha, has neither sufficient will or consciousness to enter the final stages of enlightenment, *nor sufficient consciousness to perceive that the object representative of material existence contains, or in reality is, the Spiritual dimension.*

The object representing you, the woman I desire, is of course your body, the physical illusion masking the Spirit within. Karma and Samsara belong to the physical, and illusory, world of existence, which is ruled by cause and effect, or the chain reaction that constitutes its mechanism and keeps it locked in upon itself. The chain reaction, or karma, prevents man perceiving the Spirit within matter, for, locked in upon himself, he cannot see beyond, or within. It is this Spirit within matter that holds the secret, or answer to our problem. *For Spirit itself cannot be seen; therefore man denies it; therefore I desire your body, not You, or your Spiritual essence.* The whole question hovers around sexuality, the combination of Spirit and Flesh, or body. For as swell as containing Spirit, the flesh, or matter (the body) *is contained by* Spirit. Do not imagine, then, that Spirit is in any way physical, or has any physical attributes: it is not a physical vessel;

nevertheless it is an *immaterial* vessel, being the all-containing Mind.

Whether cosmic or individual, Mind is the sacred and immaterial artefact that constantly converts itself from inner into outer and from outer into inner; the internal and external minds constitute the fundamental paradox of existence, conducting a perpetual game of charades in the existential theatre. Internal and external, or essence and existence, while both forming existence itself, i.e. the *combination* of essence and existence, *are each subordinate to, and included within, Mind, or Essence, the all-containing inner Vessel.*

Mind consists of the two co-ordinates of consciousness and unconsciousness, i.e. the spiritual and the material; sunk within Nature, the unconscious is saturated by materiality or physicality, but therein lies a paradox: the material, or unconscious, world contains spirit, or consciousness, while the spiritual, or conscious, world contains materiality, or unconsciousness. Thus the state of Unity, or material unconsciousness, contains the state of separation, or spiritual consciousness, and vice versa. *But this paradox can only be perceived consciously;* for it reveals the ideal condition of *conscious* Unity – the dimension to which the Buddhist makes his escape – within which the world of *unconscious* separation is incorporated.

This multiple paradox needs to be explained. Consciousness cannot be understood without unconsciousness, spirituality cannot be understood without materiality, separation cannot be understood without unity. The state of unity found within Nature, or the unconscious mind, is an emanation, or projection, from the divine state of unity, at the origin of Creation – way out in the Cosmos – which *contains* Nature, or the *unconscious* state of unity; the state of separation found within civilisation, or the conscious mind, is also an emanation, or projection, from the divine state of separation at the origin of Creation - way out in the Cosmos – which *contains* civilisation, or the *conscious* state of separation. *The ultimate reconciliation, therefore, is that of the Divine Origin with its existential, or material, projection.*

For we are hereby lodged within the Eternal Present – the combination of time and timeless, in which past is combined with future in the here and now; *here is revealed to the Buddha the reality of the 'world beyond', which contains the world of existence lying here in immediacy.*

No longer need we escape to the unity of the world beyond, for we find it here, within the separation of the present world. *Conscious* unity is combined with *unconscious* unity, *conscious* separation is combined with *unconscious* separation, realised by the 'immediate-now' of the Neo-Christian version of Nirvana, and symbolised in the eternally reconciling Cross.

*****

The immediate-now, or Eternal-Present, is represented, in the Cross, by the outstretched arms of Christ as he endures the frightful tension of the divorced Opposites; he suffers, for man, man's own state of schizophrenia, the riven dichotomy of what was originally the Universal Schism, a benign and positive *separation* of Opposites. The Buddha would *escape* separation, but Christ enjoins it upon us, *for without it there is no consciousness.* True consciousness is unknown to Buddhism, for the simple reason that it does not know *un*consciousness, either; neither state of awareness can exist without the other, except in an incomplete and ineffectual form; be aware of paradox, the foundation of Creation. Consciousness, in the true sense of the word, does not signify within the Buddhist way of life *because it is not separated from unconsciousness;* consciousness and unconsciousness can only co-exist in the separated state: in a state of unity, *neither* would exist, except in indistinguishable identification. *The Buddha is an intuitive,* such thought as he manifests being logical but not truly rational; although intuition *contains* reason, it is not *separated* from it, and therefore neither exists.

We can only find freedom, that is true consciousness, through individuality, i.e. plurality, or multiplicity – a thing which Buddhism is sworn against. However, individuality, or plurality, implies unity – *the harmony of the various parts of the unit.* In this case, the unit is the individual psyche, which, to be individual, must be harmonised, or unified; that is to say, it must achieve a *union* of all its parts, or functions; *unity* must give way to *union*, or *separated* unity.

Individuality, *or the unique self,* may well join the Universal Self – the goal of the Buddhist, in which the individual self is dissolved – but it will remain itself, and intact.

In bringing down the universal , or the heavenly state of unity, to the particular, or existence, the Bodhisattva, or potential Buddha, and his future apostles, or bodhisattvas, perform the ultimate reconciliation, or *Mysterium Conjunctionis* - the Mystical Union of Opposites. In the union of unity and existence, the latter of which may be regarded as the state of separation, the final condition of *separated-unity* is realised – that is to say, simultaneously *seen* and *experienced.* For Nirvana combines seeing with experiencing, - or seeing with being; *that is, consciousness with unconsciousness.*

Conscious experience, the resultant hybrid, is in fact

the combination of the spiritual and material – or, of course, unity and existence. It is in this hybrid, or paradox, of spirit and matter (materiality) that we find the solution to karma, or cause and effect – epitomised by birth and death.

How many births, how many deaths, are required before karma is exhausted? For karma goes on to infinity. How do we transmute The Many Lives into The One Life? For by doing so we deprive karma of its necessary multiplicity, or plurality, by which it is perpetuated. Sever cause from effect and you obviate multiplicity: unity remains – that is, oneness. Thus, by separation we obviate multiplicity; but separation creates a relationship, whereas multiplicity is a series of *unrelated* events. These events would, however, be related by cause and effect; but in driving a wedge between these two we create a relationship by separation, *in other words a separated unity.*

What happens to cause and effect in a separated unity? The relationship thus entailed does two things; it both separates and unites, and in this reciprocal schism, or mutual separation, we have the hope of resolution. For, in separating, or severing, cause from effect, we nullify their *unconscious relationship;* and, at the same time, we establish a *conscious* relationship, a separated-unit existing only in consciousness.

Let us, then, grasp cause and effect and, instead of obviating them, incorporate them into the state of Union, where, as we know, separation co-exists with unity. The world of existence, therefore, or the condition of cause and effect, is raised up to the world of unity, or oneness, while the world of unity is brought down to the world of existence, or multiplicity, the two worlds being combined as 'the kingdom of heaven on earth'.

The Biblical prophecy is thus proved true, and all births and deaths are united as one: The One Within The Many, or The Many Within The One.

*****

Death is the effect of birth, and birth is the effect of death – a fact well-known in Hindu and Buddhist countries, but lacking acknowledgement in the West – *because we cannot see the hidden connection between death and re-birth;* the world beyond is invisible, and although our instincts, or intuitions, tell us it exists, our logic insists that one plus one makes two and that nothing can occur between the two ends of this relationship. But two is the resulting sum, not the process of addition, which would tell us, if we let it, that one plus one adds up to anything between zero and infinity: *the in-between, or the relationship itself, regardless of the relating factors, or digits, is infinitely contracted or infinitely expanded; that is the reality of the world between the opposites.*

Cause and effect, or birth and death, are therefore nullified by their own relating factors.

We find liberation from the world of existence, or cause and effect, *by entering the relationship between the opposites,* which takes us to the world beyond; but if it were not for the opposites themselves, the raw material of this creative process, we would not have an existence from which to free ourselves – *or, more to the point, to which we may marry ourselves. There is no freedom or independence other than in union or relationship; freedom is mutual dependence.*

The Brotherhood of Man obliges us to find union across the board – with *all* communities; this is the Christian, Muslim and Buddhist code, realised today through the idea born of the Crucifixion.

*****

The above exposition has, in essence, been one of *psychological integration,* a combination of prior differentiation and subsequent harmonisation, or separation and subsequent unification. Otherwise expressed as disintegration prior to re-integration, the general process of 'integration' consists, first, of the 'separating out' of the psychological functions, or their associated psychological co-ordinates, and then of their recombining in a totally new and unique product called individuality. Individuality means, literally, separation, or dis-integration, but it is also a term applied generally to the *re*-integrated state of individual, or self.

Individuality in fact includes both dis-integration and re-integration, and therefore consists of the schism between the two halves of the self, ie subject and object, which are simultaneously dis-integrated and re-integrated by consciousness – in the first instance by putative, or primitive, consciousness, and in the second instance by transcendental consciousness. Putative consciousness is the status quo of civilisation, even today, resulting from the Fall, or Adam's disgrace, and never having developed; but ideally it would progress into transcendental consciousness in the ongoing process of individuation, or the cultivation of individuality.

Individuation is thus a creative process primarily involving the simultaneous separation, or dis-integration, and harmonisation, or re-integration, of subject and object – or self and other-than-self. Putative, *or egoic*, consciousness is located within the screen of consciousness mid-way between subject, or self, and object, or other-than-self. A diagram would be appropriate:

PSYCHE OR SELF

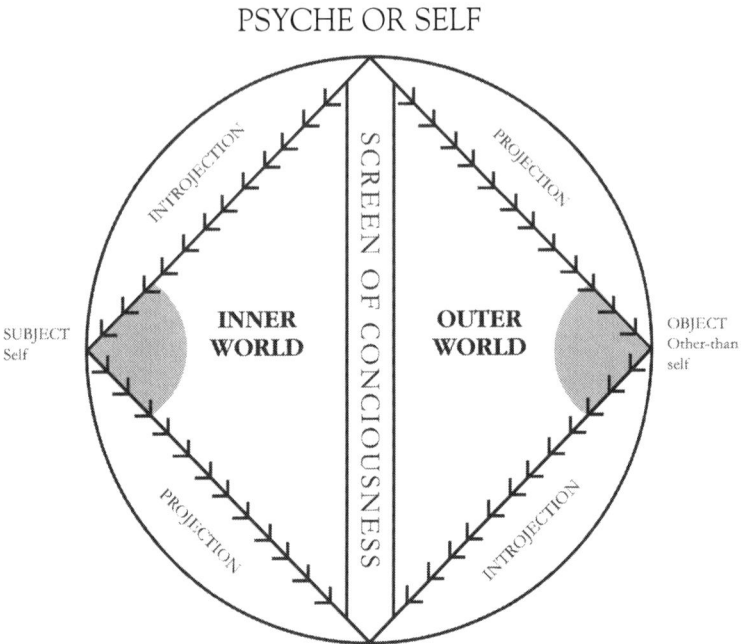

The inner world of the self and the outer world of the self correspond to the subjective and objective worlds, or those of the self and other-than-self – in which self and other-than-self simultaneously coincide and diverge, or unify and separate; thus proceeds the game of charades played by the inner and outer worlds, in the theatre of existence.

The separation and unification (or harmonisation) – in other words, dis-integration and re-integration – of the subjective and objective worlds therefore constitutes the disintegrating-reintegrating process of the self, *or individual psyche* – in other words the general process of integration, or individuation. Parallel to the integration of the subjective and objective factors is the integration of the *psychological functions*, as in the Jungian system; but we are not directly concerned with that here. However, within the relationship of inner and outer we are deeply concerned with Jung's associated system of introjection-projection, or introversion-extroversion.

Introversion introjects, or attracts, to itself – in other words, it unifies or consolidates – while extroversion projects, or repels, *from* itself; in other words, it separates or dis-establishes; thus introversion-extroversion is the principle behind disintegration-reintegration. But to go further into the mysteries of this arcane principle would exceed our purposes. Suffice it to say that its two co-ordinates work together both simultaneously and reciprocally, being the thesis and antithesis at the basis of the universal, or cosmic Paradox, i.e. the mutual and coinciding separation-unification, or identification, of the subjective and objective worlds – undergoing further integration as separated identification, or identified-separation.

Integration, or relationship, is the essence, or reality, of the psyche, whether cosmic or individual.

Furthermore, integration is both the 'in-between', or the *relationship* between, and the *relating factors themselves*, i.e. subject and object.

The opposites, or co-ordinates of the psyche, are those of subject and object and those of consciousness and unconsciousness; both pairs of opposites are related - that is, separated and identified – *by desire*, whose infrastructure centres on extroversion-introversion. Desire is the will to have, or to possess; therefore, in desiring You, I will to possess You; in other words, I will to project my self, or my consciousness, into You, while at the same time introjecting your self, or your consciousness, into myself. You, on your part, simultaneously reciprocate with your own projection-introjection.

This is the hidden reality of desire and sexual relationships; the urge to know, or be conscious of, 'the other'; carnal and spiritual knowledge of each other is what we share. Consciousness born of Love gives us *freedom* from desire, such consciousness having been *converted* from desire.

The basic means of converting desire into consciousness – the ultimate act of transubstantiation – is the prophet's recommended, and well tried, *self-suppression*, that is, *sexual* suppression, or the deliberate *frustration* of desire, as we have seen. The eventual development of consciousness, plus the development of will, results in *conscious-will*, the qualification of the Conscious Being, or unique, individual self, in whom both consciousness and will find liberation; far from losing one's self in *unity* with the Cosmic Self, one creates it in the state of *union, or separated-identification*, with that Self, where its individuality and independence are preserved.

The apocalyptic revelation inspiring this account is that of *Union in contrast to Unity*; for the *Unity* undoubtedly forming the ground of the Cosmos, or Creation itself, is at the present time being converted into the *Union* of Creation with its created projection – existence.

Unity, however, persists as the reality of the Spiritual world, by entering which the adept, whether Buddhist or Christian, obviates the plurality of cause and effect; at the same time the adept purges existence of its one-sided separation (of opposites) and establishes the reality of separated-identification, or Union. Thus the Spiritual and Material worlds are at last re-united, or re-integrated, in liberated consciousness.

*****

The re-integrated, individual self cannot, by its naturally gregarious and totally vulnerable character, exist in dissociation from either its own integral parts, or from the immediate or wider society of which it is itself an integral part; by extension, of course, the 'wider society' means the whole of civilisation. So we see what is at stake in the proposed dis-unification, or general enfranchisement, of world society.

Without universal integration, no individual state will survive in modern civilisation; nor can my proposition of 'world-consciousness' have any hope of emergence. Release from karma can only be won by the paramount psychological functions of thinking and intuition, i.e. consciousness – specifically transcendental consciousness; this is both the means and goal of the 'road to enlightenment', or the gradual awakening culminating in the ultimate and sole freedom of Nirvana.

In the state of Nirvana, however, the Buddhist would forfeit his self, while the neo-Christian adept on the contrary, would, in attaining Anthony Hill's version of Nirvana, *find* his self in all its glory, amidst *union* with the universal, or cosmic, Self, "whose service is perfect freedom".

Forthcoming Titles by Anthony Wakefield Hill

(written, but awaiting publication)

12. Schizophrenia - Perversion of the Universal Schism
    (2 volumes)

13. Parsifal's Journal, Issue II: Neo-Christian Metaphysics in the
    Second Millennium

14. The Revolutionising of Medical Procedure,
    Physical and Mental: an Outline

15. An Oblique Approach to Wagnerian Psychology: an
    Investigation into its Implications

16. Woman: Mother and Whore, Man: Father and Rake -
    A Sequel To 'The Sanctity And Profanity Of Sexuality'

17. Art Through Knowledge, Knowledge Through Art, A
    Practical Artistic And Philosophical Synthesis with Step by
    Step Instructions

18. Professor Anthony's Casebook: Pursuing The Mother,
    Pursuing The Father, A Novel Concerning a Young Couple's
    Search for their Sexual Identity

19. Parsifal's Journal, Issue III: Neo-Christian Metaphysics in the Second Millennium

20. Through Neo-Christian Eyes: the Integration of World Religions

21. The Autobiography of Anthony Hill: The Man in the Iron Mask

22. The Cosmos and Planet Earth: a Brief Survey

23. Parsifal's Journal, Issue IV, Neo-Christian Metaphysics in the Second Millennium

24. The Sphere, a Dramatic Sequel to Wagner's Ring Cycle

25. The Spirit in Man's Psyche - A Psychological Evocation of the Creative Spirit in Art, Religion and Philosophy

26. The Birth of the Psyche

27. The Death and Re-Birth of Physical Existence: Consciousness Integrated with Unconsciousness

28. Professor Anthony's Casebook: Psyche of a Whore, a Tragedy Relieved by Love

29. A Saga of Knickers, The Continuing Story of Integration

30. The Cosmic Sphere: Man's New Symbol

31. Sex Without Love is Dirty: Why You Are a Useless Lover

32. Hidden Man and Woman: Unacknowledged Evil, A Sequel to Self-Redemption

33. The Real Motives for Scottish And Catalan Independence: The Myth Of Freedom (delete?)

34. The Fall of Man: How Paradise was Lost and May be Regained

35. Even The Purest Must Become Vile: Sexual Relations

36. The Pursuit of Beauty in Art And Love: Beauty as Therapy

37. Professor Anthony's Casebook: The Road to Mandalay, An Erotically Philosophical Novel

38. The Third Element: Sequel to Ouspensky's Tertium Organum

39. Cosmic Relativity: Consciousness and Unconsciousness

40. The Illusions of Loveless Sex: How Your Dirtiness Can Be Redeemed

41. The Mind Contains the Body: a Re-Orientation of World Consciousness

42. The Holy Fool and the One Woman, a Drama Both Sacred and Profane

43. Suppression in High Places: Skulduggery by the Home Secretary and Others

44. Centripetality-Centrifugality; An Augmentation of Jung's Introversion-Extroversion

45. Karma Revisited: Predictability as in Coronation Street

46. The Trollope's Way, a Tale of Perverted Love

47. Love and the Third Woman, a Sequel to 'The Trollope's Way'

48. Energy and Consciousness, the Threshold of Perception

49. Line and Perception, Featuring the One Woman and Individual Woman

50. Why Spirit is the Only Reality, Featuring La Fille D'Energie

Printed in Poland
by Amazon Fulfillment
Poland Sp. z o.o., Wrocław